Survival Guides You Didn't Know You Needed

SURVIVING
AN ALIEN ATTACK

Thomas Kingsley Troupe

BLACK RABBIT BOOKS

Hi Jinx is published by Black Rabbit Books
P.O. Box 3263, Mankato, Minnesota, 56002.
www.blackrabbitbooks.com
Copyright © 2018 Black Rabbit Books

Marysa Storm, editor; Michael Sellner, designer;
Catherine Cates, production designer;
Omay Ayres, photo researcher

Library of Congress Cataloging-in-Publication Data
Names: Troupe, Thomas Kingsley, author.
Title: Surviving an alien attack / by Thomas Kingsley
Troupe.
Description: Mankato, Minnesota : Black Rabbit Books,
[2018] |
Series: Hi jinx. Survival guides you didn't know you needed |
Includes bibliographical references and index.
Identifiers: LCCN 2017007263 (print) | LCCN 2017024684
(ebook) | ISBN 9781680723694 (e-book) | ISBN
9781680723397 (library binding)
Subjects: LCSH: Extraterrestrial beings–Juvenile humor. |
Unidentified flying objects–Juvenile humor. | Human-alien
encounters–Juvenile humor. Classification: LCC PN6231.E97
(ebook) | LCC PN6231.E97 T76 2018 (print) | DDC 818/.602–
dc23
LC record available at https://lccn.loc.gov/2017007263

Printed in China. 9/17

Image Credits

CONTENTS

Dear Reader,

To be honest, the author's **manuscript** wasn't supposed to become a book. There was a horrible mix up. You can keep reading, if you want. Just don't take any of these suggestions seriously.

Sincerely,
a very sorry editor

Chapter 1
STARGAZING
GONE WRONG

The night sky is still and quiet. Stars twinkle from light-years away. The moon shines brightly. All is right in the world.

But wait! Those big bright stars are getting closer. They're not stars. They're spaceships! Aliens have arrived. It could happen, you know. Aliens could invade Earth.*

*Editor's Note: Does the author think rabbits are aliens? He was hired to write a book about rabbits.

Time to Survive!

The spaceships have giant lasers.
The aliens have creepy eyes and big
heads. Their ray guns can turn people
to ash and melt cities.

Thankfully, you're prepared. You've
got a survival guide you never thought
you'd need. It's time to survive an
alien attack!

Places with Many UFO Sightings

Myrtle Beach (in South Carolina, United States)

The M-Triangle (in the Ural Mountains, Russia)

Salisbury Plain (in Wiltshire, United Kingdom)

The Welsh Triangle (in Dyfed, Wales)

*Editor's Note: This is absolutely ridiculous.

8

Chapter 2

MAKE A PEACE OFFERING

What's one thing all aliens have in common? Aliens don't wear pants! Can you think of a single alien sighting that mentions alien clothing?

Use this info to confuse the space monsters. Just offer them pants. They'll be too busy tripping over the **slacks** to chase you.*

Survival List   Types of Pants to Offer

jeans   yoga pants

capris   bell-bottoms

Sandwich

An alien's diet must be disgusting. Just think about it. They probably eat **fungus** or 12-eyed Goppelux bugs. Hamburgers don't exist in outer space.

Offer them an Earth treat. Aliens love sandwiches. Give them some turkey melts with extra mayo. The food will warm the aliens' glowing hearts.

Survival List

Condiments Aliens Might Like

spicy mustard
low-fat mayo
relish

Goppelux bug

11

Survival List
Things To Bring on a Sub
submarine sandwiches
taco shells
(You'll need them for taco night.)
board games
books

*Editor's Note: This idea is crazy. How many people do you know who have a sub?

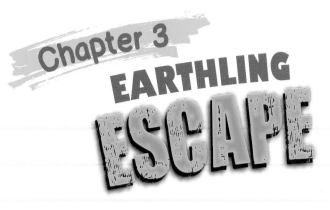

Chapter 3
EARTHLING ESCAPE

The best way to survive may be to escape. Look around your neighborhood. Surely there's a submarine you can borrow.*

Movies have taught us that aliens hate Earth's water. It makes them sick. It cleans them off too. So go explore the sea. You can surface when the attack wraps up.

Caves

Surviving might mean going back to basics. Run to the nearest cave. Live like your **ancestors** once did.

Aliens think we only live in cities and houses. They would never think to look in a cold, chilly cave. Stay in the cave until the fighting is over.

The world's largest cave is in Vietnam. It's so big that it has its own **climate**.

Chapter 4
FIGHT FOR YOUR LIFE

Sick of fleeing? Maybe it's time to fight back. Do the aliens have **tentacles**? If so, you're in luck.

Put your knot-tying skills to work. Sneak up behind the aliens. Then tie their tentacles together. Laugh as the creatures fall to the ground.

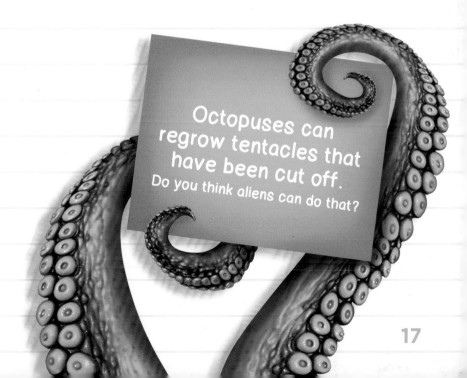

Octopuses can regrow tentacles that have been cut off. Do you think aliens can do that?

Invade Them!

Maybe the only solution is to invade the invaders. Simply board a spaceship. Then head for the stars.*

Imagine the aliens' surprise when you come to their planet. Blow up their cities! Watch them run for the caves!

You can't know for sure when the aliens will come. It could be years from now. Or it could be next Tuesday. But with this guide, you can face an alien attack!

*Editor's Note: This is also crazy. Finding a spaceship would be even harder than finding a sub.

Chapter 5
GET IN ON THE
HI JINX

An alien attack may seem ridiculous. But there are many people who believe aliens exist. Former astronaut Dr. Edgar Mitchell believes in aliens. He thinks they've been watching Earth for a long time.

Take It One Step More

1. The universe is a giant place. Do you think there are aliens out there? Why or why not?

2. What should Earth's first step be if aliens visited?

3. What do you think the author of this book was thinking? If his suggestions are crazy, why did he write the book?

GLOSSARY

ancestor (AN-ses-ter)—a person who was in someone's family in past times

climate (KLAHY-mit)—the usual weather conditions in a particular place or region

condiment (KON-duh-muhnt)—something that is added to food to give it more flavor

fungus (FUN-gus)—a living thing, similar to a plant that has no flowers, that lives on dead or decaying things

manuscript (MAN-yuh-skript)—the original copy of a book before it has been printed

slacks (SLAKS)—dress pants

tentacle (TEN-tuh-kuhl)—a long, flexible arm that some animals have

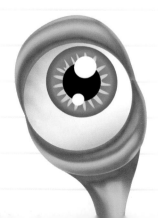

BOOKS

Anderson, Amy, and Brian Anderson. *Space Dictionary for Kids: The Everything Guide for Kids Who Love Space.* Waco, TX: Prufrock Press Inc., 2016.

Becker, Helaine. *Everything Space.* Everything Series. Washington, D.C.: National Geographic Society, 2015.

Noll, Elizabeth. *UFOs.* Strange … but True? Mankato, MN: Black Rabbit Books, 2017.

WEBSITES

Are We Alone?
**www.esa.int/esaKIDSen/
Arewealone.html**

Do Aliens Really Exist?
**discoverykids.com/articles/
do-aliens-really-exist/**

NASA Kids' Club
www.nasa.gov/kidsclub/index.html

A

astronauts, 20

C

caves, 14, 15, 18

F

food, 10, 12

O

octopuses, 17

S

stars, 5, 18

submarines, 12, 13

U

UFO sightings, 7, 9